REFLECTIONS ON THE BIRTH OF CHRIST

RE-DISCOVERING THE WONDER IN LUKE 1 & 2

AIMEE MAE WILEY

Reflections on the Birth of Christ

Re-Discovering the Wonder in Luke 1 & 2

Aimee Mae Wiley

All Rights Reserved

ISBN: 9781731012692

Editing, formatting & cover design by Reverie Press

"LOOK FOR THE WONDER."

Earlier this fall, the Holy Spirit directed me to read through the book of Luke. I was feeling stagnant in my relationship with the Lord, to the point of doubting my faith. Returning to this gospel account to rekindle my relationship with Him seemed like a good place to start.

I began reading the familiar birth story of Jesus found in Luke 1-2 and briefly considered skipping it. After all, I already knew the story inside and out, and besides, it was September, not December. I could always go back and revisit it later. It was at this moment the Lord prompted me with the thought, "Look for the wonder." That was all it took for me to be all in on this journey. I committed to read Luke 1-2 (and the subsequent chapters) with fresh eyes and to look for the wonder, as the Lord instructed.

What I discovered is that, although familiar, there is nothing commonplace or ordinary about the birth of Christ. Every verse overflows with the wonder of God. Reading His holy words led me to worship Him once more and to praise Him for all He has done and continues to do.

Have you been waiting for an answer to prayer for days, weeks, or even years? Do you feel abandoned or forgotten?

Have you been shamed or disgraced for something outside your control? Do you struggle with trusting God in the details of life?

Are you young and wondering if God has a plan for your life? Or, are you older and wondering if there is anything more God can do through you? Do you want to surrender your life to God but feel nervous about what it might entail?

If you answered yes to any of these questions, know you are not alone. The people you will encounter in these first two chapters of Luke are not so different from you and me. They faced the same struggles we do, only within a different historical and cultural context. God met each of them in a personal way and brought "*good news of great joy for all the people*"—that includes you and me!

This devotional is an invitation to join me on the journey I took to rediscover the wonder of our Lord's birth and the events leading up to it. Rejoice with Mary, Elizabeth, the shepherds, and all those who chose to believe that a newborn babe could be the Savior of the world.

LUKE 1:1-4

A BRIEF INTRODUCTION

¹ Many have undertaken to draw up an account of the things that have been fulfilled among us, ² just as they were handed down to us by those who from the first were eyewitnesses and servants of the word. ³ With this in mind, since I myself have carefully investigated everything from the beginning, I too decided to write an orderly account for you, most excellent Theophilus, ⁴ so that you may know the certainty of the things you have been taught.

As we begin, it is important to understand both who the author of this book was, as well as the recipient for whom it was intended. It is clear from the first two verses of Luke that the story of Jesus was quite popular. He was the subject of many writings, not just those found in the New Testament. Although Luke was not one of the original apostles, he did meet and gather eyewitness accounts from those who had walked with Jesus. His occupation as a doctor would naturally have led him to be both skeptical and thorough in his analysis of Jesus' life and claims to be the Son of God.

As a Gentile, Luke would have had to study the history and culture of the Jewish people to provide the detailed descriptions he gives in his account. He even assures us of this in verse three: *"I myself have carefully investigated everything from the beginning."* What I appreciate about Luke is his commitment to providing an orderly account based on his findings. His desire was to help those searching for truth to *"know the certainty"* of who Jesus was.

There are many ideas surrounding the personage of Theophilus, to whom Luke writes the books of both Luke and Acts. I always thought Theophilus was not so much a specific person as it was a name intended to include the greater community of believers. However, this may not be the case. The name Theophilus means "loved by God" which is akin to being called "friend of God." That Luke addresses him as *"most excellent Theophilus"* indicates he was more likely an actual individual and probably one of higher rank. He could have been a Roman official or wealthy patron. Less likely, he could also have been a Jewish priest.

Whoever Theophilus was, we can conclude with certainty that he was "an individual interested in the gospel. His importance lies in the fact that he was the original recipient of two magnificent pieces of inspired literature." † Moreover, I don't think his name was accidental or arbitrary. The book of Luke is for all those who seek to know the truth and to know Jesus more fully. It is for all of us, because we are all loved by God.

A Prayer for Today

～

Lord, as I open Your Word to read the orderly account of Your birth recorded by Luke, may I do so with my mind and heart open to the wonder of how You came to earth as a human baby in order to demonstrate Your love for me by dying on the Cross. Thank You for the gift of Your Word and eternal life.

LUKE 1:5-7

THE WONDER OF FAITHFULNESS

⁵ In the time of Herod king of Judea there was a priest named Zechariah, who belonged to the priestly division of Abijah; his wife Elizabeth was also a descendant of Aaron. ⁶ Both of them were righteous in the sight of God, observing all the Lord's commands and decrees blamelessly. ⁷ But they were childless because Elizabeth was not able to conceive, and they were both very old.

The first sign of wonder I find in the birth story of Jesus is this: God never fails to keep His promises. Look at how, multiple generations after God established Aaron as head of the priestly line, the Levites are still intact and trackable. Luke designates both Zechariah and Elizabeth here as descendants of Aaron.

People today try to trace their family trees, but how far back can they really go, even with all the technology we have? I'm going to throw out 700 years as a guess, based on accounts I have read. Only God can trace all the way back to the beginning of humanity, and more specifically, the 1500-plus years between Aaron and Zechariah. He had a plan from the beginning of time, and nothing and no one could thwart it.

Next, look at how this older couple is described: *"Both of them were righteous in the sight of God, observing* all *the Lord's commands and decrees blamelessly."* Here is a couple who committed themselves to pleasing the Lord in all they did. They were not young and idealistic. They were *"very old."* They had lived through a lifetime of trials, sicknesses, struggles, and sorrow *("they were childless because Elizabeth was not able to conceive"),* yet they did not abandon their trust in God but remained faithful to Him throughout decades of barrenness.

Although highly regarded for the honorable way they lived their lives, Zechariah and Elizabeth still would have been disgraced for their inability to bear children. A fruitful womb was a mark of blessing from the Lord. Even without God's visible blessing, though, they continued to keep the Lord's commands without wavering. Ultimately, God chose them to be part of His incredible plan to enter our world through the person of His Son, Jesus Christ.

Even more amazing was that they lived with such steadfast devotion during a time of spiritual dryness. There had been no audible or prophetic voice of God for approximately 400 years.

Zechariah and Elizabeth were living by faith in a God they could not see or hear, known only from the Law, which had been passed down from generation to generation.

We have the Holy Spirit living inside us, and still we stumble at the slightest obstacle. We have easy access to God's Word, and yet we neglect it and go our own way. Who among us can call ourselves righteous and blameless, apart from the work of Christ in our lives?

A Prayer for Today

Lord, help me to remain faithful as I wait for Your return and to be upright in my daily walk with You, so I can be part of Your greater plan as it unfolds.

LUKE 1:8-10

THE WONDER OF BEING CHOSEN

⁸ Once when Zechariah's division was on duty and he was serving as priest before God, ⁹ he was chosen by lot, according to the custom of the priesthood, to go into the temple of the Lord and burn incense. ¹⁰ And when the time for the burning of incense came, all the assembled worshipers were praying outside.

Zechariah was chosen by lot to enter the temple and burn incense. The Levites still regarded these seemingly ritualistic daily duties with awe and reverence. They had continued to follow the commandments laid down centuries before, even after years of hearing nothing from God. Oswald Chambers calls it "remaining steadfast in silence."‡

What was Zechariah expecting that fateful day? He had come from his hometown in Judea to perform his priestly duties for two weeks. Was he simply there to faithfully do his job as he had for decades past? Did he have a sense of expectation when the lots were drawn, or had he given up hope of ever entering the inner court of the temple?

Lots were drawn twice each day for the services performed in the temple, which included: removing the ashes, bringing the pan of burning coals, and burning incense. That day,

Zechariah drew the most important job of all—the burning of incense, which was symbolic of the prayers of the people.§

Scholars think there were approximately 20,000 priests at the time, so each priest had a once in a lifetime chance of being chosen to enter the Holy Place to burn incense. Zechariah had waited his whole priestly life for this moment. What was going through his mind as he carried the incense into the Holy Place? Whatever his posture was upon entering the temple that day, Zechariah had no idea what awaited him.

A Prayer for Today

Lord, the routines and rhythms of life are not without their value. Even in the mundane moments, I can experience Your glory. Help me to live in anticipation of what You will do with my ordinary life to make it extraordinary for You.

LUKE 1:11-13

THE WONDER OF BEING CALLED BY NAME

[11] Then an angel of the Lord appeared to him, standing at the right side of the altar of incense. [12] When Zechariah saw him, he was startled and was gripped with fear. [13] But the angel said to him: "Do not be afraid, Zechariah; your prayer has been heard. Your wife Elizabeth will bear you a son, and you are to call him John.

An angel! A real, live, terrifying angel awaited Zechariah as he approached the altar. We have all been startled by an unexpected presence, but few of us have been *"gripped with fear"* like Zechariah. Recently, I entered the restroom at church as a friend exited. She was more than startled; she was gripped with fear. She explained how her inordinate fear of being startled stemmed from being mugged years earlier. To this day, when she encounters someone unexpectedly, that primal fear still lingers—a kind of PTSD.

In Zechariah's case, his fear likely stemmed from his awareness of Gabriel's imposing presence and holiness in the light of his own sinfulness. We cannot stand before that which is holy without reverent fear.

However, there is also beauty and wonder in this moment.

Catch Gabriel's encouraging greeting: *"Do not be afraid, Zechariah."* This is no arbitrary meeting; Zechariah drew his lot according to the will of God. God sent Gabriel that day to speak directly to none other than Zechariah.

Then he says, *"Your prayer has been heard."* What prayer? The rest of the verse reveals the prayer of Zechariah's heart: to have a son. How many years did he pray this prayer? Did he finally stop once age became a barrier to possibility? His response in verse 18 seems to imply this was the case.

How often do we give up on our dreams? How often do we stop praying and believing because it seems like our chance has passed? How often do we put limitations on God's power? This divine encounter shows us, like we read in Isaiah 55:8-9, that God's ways are higher than our ways, and His thoughts are higher than our thoughts. God's timing rarely matches up with our own, but He is always faithful to answer.

Finally, Gabriel eliminates any confusion as to who will be having this baby and what his name will be. Unlike other stories in the Old Testament—where people took matters into their own hands (e.g., Sarah, Rachel, etc.)—there will be no surrogate mother for this child. Aged Elizabeth will bear Zechariah's son, and they will name him John, which means "God is gracious." God's grace is extended not only to them in providing a son, but also to the entire human race in providing salvation through His Son!

A Prayer for Today

Lord, you know the desire of my heart. You hear the prayers I have offered day after day, year after year, for a dream, a loved one, a hurting soul, or a wayward child. It may seem like You are silent, but in this passage, I can take hope in the truth that You are listening, caring, and preparing a way where there seems to be no way. It says in Ephesians 3:20-21 that you are able to do exceedingly and abundantly more than I can ask or think, and I am going to cling to that promise as I wait.

THE WONDER OF PURPOSE

¹⁴ He will be a joy and delight to you, and many will rejoice because of his birth, ¹⁵ for he will be great in the sight of the Lord. He is never to take wine or other fermented drink, and he will be filled with the Holy Spirit even before he is born. ¹⁶ He will bring back many of the people of Israel to the Lord their God. ¹⁷ And he will go on before the Lord, in the spirit and power of Elijah, to turn the hearts of the parents to their children and the disobedient to the wisdom of the righteous—to make ready a people prepared for the Lord."

As a mother, I can only imagine this moment for Zechariah. Not only is he being promised a son, but this angel is describing him as *"a joy and delight."* I always feel both proud and humbled when someone tells me something good my child has said or done, especially when it comes from a person whose opinion I respect.

To have a child be called *"great in the sight of the Lord"* by an angel from heaven, though, would be the ultimate, most unimaginable praise! How strange and wonderful it must have been to hear Gabriel explain the life Zechariah's son would lead!

John would one day go before the Lord in the spirit of Elijah and lead the people back to God. Elijah was one of the most illustrious prophets of the Old Testament. Now, Zechariah's long-awaited son will become a prophet of the same caliber as Elijah with a divine commission to *"make ready a people prepared for the Lord."*

After all these years of silence, a prophet is coming, and he will be Zechariah's son! It is all too much for Zechariah to take in, as we will see in the continuing passage.

A Prayer for Today

~

Lord, help me to live with expectation and joy for what you have planned and to be ready to join in Your amazing, life-saving work in the world.

LUKE 1:18-20

THE WONDER OF THE UNBELIEVABLE

18 Zechariah asked the angel, "How can I be sure of this? I am an old man and my wife is well along in years."

19 The angel said to him, "I am Gabriel. I stand in the presence of God, and I have been sent to speak to you and to tell you this good news. 20 And now you will be silent and not able to speak until the day this happens, because you did not believe my words, which will come true at their appointed time."

It is almost comical to think of Zechariah responding the way he does. Gabriel has just laid out a detailed plan of events for John, and all Zechariah can think of is how old he and Elizabeth are! He questions the logistics of pregnancy and childbirth, given their advanced ages. The idea certainly does sound outlandish, but this is no laughing matter. It is imperative that Zechariah continues to walk in obedience to the Lord, especially now, or John will not be born, and God's plan will not prevail (which, of course, we all know is impossible).

I imagine Gabriel pulling himself up to his full, majestic, glorious height and angelic brilliance as he states with a booming voice (like that of the great Oz), *"I am Gabriel, and I stand in the presence of God, and I have been sent to speak to you and to tell you this good news."* To further drive the point home, he strikes Zechariah mute because he doubted the Lord's message and messenger.

A Prayer for Today

Lord, it is so easy to question that which does not make sense to my finite mind. Help me to remember that Your ways are not my ways and that I can trust You and Your Word. Keep my ears and heart open to the message You have for me, and help me to respond with immediate obedience.

THE WONDER OF WAITING

²¹ Meanwhile, the people were waiting for Zechariah and wondering why he stayed so long in the temple. ²² When he came out, he could not speak to them. They realized he had seen a vision in the temple, for he kept making signs to them but remained unable to speak.

²³ When his time of service was completed, he returned home. ²⁴ After this his wife Elizabeth became pregnant and for five months remained in seclusion. ²⁵ "The Lord has done this for me," she said. "In these days he has shown his favor and taken away my disgrace among the people."

It is apparent as Zechariah exits the temple that something extraordinary has happened. He cannot tell anyone, though, because he cannot speak, and gestures can hardly convey the significance of his encounter with Gabriel. As he has done for decades, Zechariah completes his time of service before returning home. And here is where the rubber meets the road, so to speak. Zechariah must demonstrate his faith by works.

For John to be born and fulfill his divine destiny, Zechariah has to *act* in faith: he must engage in sexual relations with his wife. Now, I am not as old as they were at the time, and I have no idea what this experience is like when one is "very old," but it had to be done. Their act of obedience results in Elizabeth becoming pregnant, a miracle in itself! Having lived under the shadow of barrenness all those years, only to find herself pregnant at the most physically challenging time of her life, Elizabeth chooses to praise God. *"The Lord has done this for me. In these days he has shown his favor and taken away my disgrace among the people."*

There is no, "Why now, Lord?" There is no reluctant obedience on her part. She has experienced the grace of God firsthand, and she is filled with joy and gratitude. Still, she remains in seclusion for five months, perhaps to ensure the viability of the pregnancy, or in quiet devotion to God.

However, once she did reveal her condition, Elizabeth and Zechariah probably became instantly famous in their town: "Barren, Elderly Couple Visited by Angel and Expecting a Baby!" I can just imagine the glow on Elizabeth's face, her smile lighting up every room she entered. She had been vindicated and blessed by the Almighty God! Her disgrace was erased by the *"grace of God."*

A Prayer for Today

~

Lord God, You say in Jeremiah 29:11, "*For I know the plans I have for you, plans to prosper you and not to harm you, plans to give you hope and a future.*" This is no more evident than in the story of Zechariah and Elizabeth. When the waiting grows long, and I feel the weight of scornfulness from those around me, help me to remember what the wait must have been like for Elizabeth, what it must have been like for You as you walked this earth. Help me to be "*joyful in hope, patient in affliction, faithful in prayer.*" (Rom. 12:12)

LUKE 1:26-33

THE WONDER OF THE UNKNOWN

²⁶ In the sixth month of Elizabeth's pregnancy, God sent the angel Gabriel to Nazareth, a town in Galilee, ²⁷ to a virgin pledged to be married to a man named Joseph, a descendant of David. The virgin's name was Mary. ²⁸ The angel went to her and said, "Greetings, you who are highly favored! The Lord is with you."

²⁹ Mary was greatly troubled at his words and wondered what kind of greeting this might be. ³⁰ But the angel said to her, "Do not be afraid, Mary; you have found favor with God. ³¹ You will conceive and give birth to a son, and you are to call him Jesus. ³² He will be great and will be called the Son of the Most High. The Lord God will give him the throne of his father David, ³³ and he will reign over Jacob's descendants forever; his kingdom will never end."

Put yourself in Mary's sandals for a moment. You are 14 years old (the customary age of betrothal at this time and place was 12-14 years of age) and preparing for your wedding. There are garments to sew and arrangements to make. Your mind is filled with wonder at the idea of marriage. What will Joseph be like as a husband? Will the home he provides for you feel as much like home as the one you are sitting in right now? Are you ready to be mistress of the house: making meals, keeping things clean and in order? How long until children arrive?

Mary might have taken everything in stride as part of the normal course of life, or she might have felt anxious and uncertain about all the unknowns. We really cannot know for sure, except for later clues into her personality, which reveal her to be a reflective, thoughtful young woman. Like Zechariah, though, there was no way for Mary to predict, as she sat in her room reflecting upon her upcoming nuptials or sewing her trousseau, that the angel Gabriel would suddenly appear in her room!

"Greetings, you who are highly favored! The Lord is with you."

The Bible says Mary was greatly troubled at his words and wondered at their meaning. I should think so. *Who is this guy? What does he mean, I am "highly favored?" How is the Lord with me?* As we have covered, God has been silent these past 400 years, His presence not even a distant memory to the people of this time.

As with Zechariah, Gabriel puts Mary at ease. *"Do not be afraid, Mary* (again, the intentional, personal use of her name*); you have found favor with God."* He then proceeds to describe Mary's part in the most sensational, wonderful plan ever created: she will give birth to the Son of God, the Savior of the world! The Jewish people have been waiting for the Messiah for thousands of years, and now Mary is going to be the catalyst to bring Him into the world.

A Prayer for Today

∾

Lord Jesus, life is filled with so many unknowns, many of which are outside our control. I cannot imagine what it must have been like for Mary the day she found out she would give birth to You, the Son of God. But, I do know what it feels like to live in uncertainty and the worry which accompanies it. Help me to remember the words of Gabriel when I face the unknowns of life: "*Do not be afraid,* [insert name]; *you have found favor with God.*" Help me to remember that I am right in the middle of Your plan for me, Lord, and that I can trust You with the details of my life.

LUKE 1:34-38

THE WONDER OF SURRENDER

^{34} "How will this be," Mary asked the angel, "since I am a virgin?"

^{35} The angel answered, "The Holy Spirit will come on you, and the power of the Most High will overshadow you. So the holy one to be born will be called the Son of God. ^{36} Even Elizabeth your relative is going to have a child in her old age, and she who was said to be unable to conceive is in her sixth month. ^{37} For nothing will be impossible with God."

^{38} "I am the Lord's servant," Mary answered. "May your word to me be fulfilled." Then the angel left her.

What I love about Mary—and perhaps it is due to her youth—is her immediate acceptance of the situation. Unlike Zechariah's *"How can I be sure of this?"* Mary asks, *"How will this be?"* Both had impossible situations: Zechariah was too old to have children, and Mary was a virgin, but Mary's response was one of curiosity, not doubt.

Gabriel explains the logistics of the situation, which are cryptic in and of themselves: *"The Holy Spirit will come on you, and the power of the Most High will overshadow you."* He then offers a tangible piece of evidence for God's plan: Elizabeth's pregnancy. Their conversation closes with two of the most faith-building, beautiful phrases in the Bible:

Gabriel: *"For nothing will be impossible with God." (ESV)*

Mary: *"I am the Lord's servant. May it be to me as you have said."*

Mary may very well be the greatest woman of faith in the Bible. Her words are reminiscent of those from the great prophet Isaiah, "Here I am. Send me." What is incredible about Mary is that she is just a young girl, not a learned scholar of the Torah, a prophet, or a priest. Her simple, obedient faith in something so extraordinary and supernatural is unparalleled. In Mary, we see the complete surrender of her will and life to the ultimate plan of God: to send Jesus the Savior into the world through her own, virginal body.

In a corresponding reading from Oswald Chambers' *My Utmost for His Highest*, he describes surrender. "Whatever is perplexing heart or mind is a call to the will. 'Come to Me.' It is a voluntary coming. 'If any man will come after Me, let him deny himself.' The surrender here is of myself to Jesus, myself with His rest at the heart of it. After surrender, what? The whole life after surrender is an aspiration for unbroken communication with God."‡

Therein are the beauty and the wonder of Mary's surrender, the voluntary giving up of her very self to God.

A Prayer for Today

~

Lord Jesus, I want to live a surrendered life, to find Your rest as I release my anxieties and burdens into Your care. You will not force me to follow; it is my choice to come, to say as Mary did, *"I am the Lord's servant. May it be to me as You have said."* Help me to recognize that Your plan is greater than any I might have for myself. I lift my hands and my heart to You today in surrender.

LUKE 1:39-45

THE WONDER OF ENCOURAGEMENT

39 At that time Mary got ready and hurried to a town in the hill country of Judea, 40 where she entered Zechariah's home and greeted Elizabeth. 41 When Elizabeth heard Mary's greeting, the baby leaped in her womb, and Elizabeth was filled with the Holy Spirit. 42 In a loud voice she exclaimed: "Blessed are you among women, and blessed is the child you will bear! 43 But why am I so favored, that the mother of my Lord should come to me? 44 As soon as the sound of your greeting reached my ears, the baby in my womb leaped for joy. 45 Blessed is she who has believed that the Lord would fulfill his promises to her!" (ESV)

Mary has a supernatural encounter with the living God which results in her carrying the very life of God within her body. Remembering what Gabriel said about her cousin Elizabeth, Mary hurries to the town of Judah to see her. Who else could understand this strange and wonderful thing that has happened?

I imagine her breathless, with flushed cheeks, bursting into Zechariah and Elizabeth's home. "Elizabeth!" she calls out as she flies through the front door. For those of us who have been pregnant, we all know and cherish those subtle moments of movement from the child within us. We may not be as excited about the constant pushing, punching, and kicking they do late in the night. However, I cannot think of a time when any of my children *leaped* in my womb like John did upon hearing Mary's greeting. The baby residing in Elizabeth's womb recognizes the voice of Mary—the mother of God the Savior—and leaps!

With no prior knowledge of Mary's condition (that we know of), Elizabeth proclaims in the Spirit a beautiful blessing over Mary, ending with "*Blessed is she who has believed that the Lord would fulfill his promises to her!*"

What an encouragement Elizabeth is! As one who is also experiencing the Lord's promises being fulfilled through her, she can see and encourage Mary's faith. There are women later in Luke (including Mary) who will remind us of this kind of joy and faith—those who walked with Jesus and rejoiced in His resurrection.

For now, though, Mary is about to face intense scrutiny from her community, justifiable divorce from her almost-husband, and potential excommunication from her family. She could even be stoned to death! What a blessed relief to spend time with Elizabeth—someone who has experienced both public shame and divine grace. Together, they are able to rejoice in the amazing part they get to play in God's cosmic plan to save the world through their sons: John, the herald; Jesus, the Savior.

(Side note: I cannot help but mention the wonder of Mary, a young girl, believing the Lord so implicitly, trusting His word, delighting in His promises. How did she become such a beautiful picture of the Christian life at such a young age? There is no mention of her upbringing or family, but I certainly would love to know more about how they raised such a remarkable young woman.)

A Prayer for Today

Lord Jesus, thank you for the gift of friendship and the encouragement it brings! In difficult seasons of life, when hard times come, people are unkind, or I feel discouraged, there is nothing like a friend who understands and can lift me up with a kind word of encouragement and prayer. Is there someone who could use an Elizabeth in their life today? Show me who it is and how I can be an encouraging friend to them.

LUKE 1:46-56

THE WONDER OF WORSHIP

Mary's Song of Praise: The Magnificat

⁴⁶ And Mary said,

"My soul magnifies the Lord,
⁴⁷ and my spirit rejoices in God my Savior,
⁴⁸ for he has looked on the humble estate of his servant.
For behold, from now on all generations will call me blessed;
⁴⁹ for he who is mighty has done great things for me,
and holy is his name.
⁵⁰ And his mercy is for those who fear him
from generation to generation.
⁵¹ He has shown strength with his arm;
he has scattered the proud in the thoughts of their hearts;
⁵² he has brought down the mighty from their thrones
and exalted those of humble estate;
⁵³ he has filled the hungry with good things,
and the rich he has sent away empty.
⁵⁴ He has helped his servant Israel,
in remembrance of his mercy,
⁵⁵ as he spoke to our fathers,

to Abraham and to his offspring forever."

⁵⁶ And Mary remained with her about three months and returned to her home. (ESV)

Mary's song serves as a model to us as believers, guiding us in our own worship and prayer. First, she praises God:

v 46,47 *My soul glorifies the Lord; my spirit rejoices in God my Savior.*

v 49 *The Mighty One has done great things for me; Holy is his name.*

Then she recalls who He is, His attributes, and all that He has done and will do.

v 50 *His* mercy extends *to those who fear him.*

v 51 *He has* performed mighty deeds *with his arm.*

v 52 *He has* brought rulers down *and* lifted up the humble.

v 53 *He has* filled the hungry *with good things and* sent the rich away *empty.*

v 54 *He has* helped Israel *and* remembered to be merciful.

v 55 *He has* kept his promises *to Abraham and all of his offspring.*

Her song is an illumination of the character of God by the direction of the Holy Spirit.

Finally, going back to the beginning, we find a key to our own lives:

v 48 "*He has been mindful of the humble state of his servant. From now on, all generations will call me blessed.*" It is only in true humility that we can be raised up to a place of honor.

A Prayer for Today

~

Lord God, Mary's song reminds me of the Psalms, recalling who You are and all that You have done for Your people. You are powerful and merciful, gracious and just. You provide and protect. You lift me up in my weakness; Your joy is my strength. I praise you, God!

LUKE 1:57-66

THE WONDER OF REJOICING

The Birth of John the Baptist

⁵⁷ Now the time came for Elizabeth to give birth, and she bore a son. ⁵⁸ And her neighbors and relatives heard that the Lord had shown great mercy to her, and they rejoiced with her. ⁵⁹ And on the eighth day they came to circumcise the child. And they would have called him Zechariah after his father, ⁶⁰ but his mother answered, "No; he shall be called John." ⁶¹ And they said to her, "None of your relatives is called by this name." ⁶² And they made signs to his father, inquiring what he wanted him to be called. ⁶³ And he asked for a writing tablet and wrote, "His name is John." And they all wondered. ⁶⁴ And immediately his mouth was opened and his tongue loosed, and he spoke, blessing God. ⁶⁵ And fear came on all their neighbors. And all these things were talked about through all the hill country of Judea, ⁶⁶ and all who heard them laid them up in their hearts, saying, "What then will this child be?" For the hand of the Lord was with him. (ESV)

When Elizabeth's neighbors and relatives heard about God's great mercy toward Elizabeth in giving her a son, they rejoiced with her, sharing in her joy. However, as I'm sure we have all experienced, it is not always this way. Do we rejoice at the success of others, or do we begrudge them and feel jealous or abandoned by God?

I know I have struggled with this as a writer, seeing my friends receive more likes and comments on their blog posts or greater opportunities for their writing. Instead of celebrating their successes with them, I have felt defeated and jealous. I have then redoubled my own efforts, only to find them falling flat because I was working from a place of comparison rather than authenticity. However, in the times I have genuinely rejoiced with my friends in their success, my own joy has been multiplied. I've felt lighter and freer to create the way God has gifted me. It is wonderful to see the support Elizabeth received during this momentous time. No one was trying to steal her joy or begrudge her of it.

Elizabeth's obedience and courage is also evident in this scene. Perhaps Zechariah had written the name John on a tablet for her. Or, maybe the Holy Spirit prompted her to state John's name at that moment. Whatever the case, she didn't back down to popular opinion or cultural customs. She spoke up and defended the name God had chosen for her son, even though there was no rhyme or reason for it.

In confirmation, Zechariah began writing John's name on his tablet, and in that moment he was unshackled from his silence. All those present were filled with wonder. "*What then is this child to become?*" they asked. No one could doubt that God's hand was on him.

(Side note: Imagine all those months of pregnancy for Zechariah and Elizabeth, not being able to talk about what the Lord had done! I'm sure Zechariah communicated in writing, but it was not nearly as convenient as being able to express their wonder and excitement in verbal conversation.)

A Prayer for Today

~

Lord, thank you for fulfilling Your purposes and keeping Your promises, as we see with the birth of John. Help me to rejoice with others when they experience successes, breakthroughs, or blessings and not to give way to jealousy and resentment.

LUKE 1:67-80

THE WONDER OF PROPHECY

Zechariah's Prophecy

⁶⁷ *And his father Zechariah was filled with the Holy Spirit and prophesied, saying,*

⁶⁸ *"Blessed be the Lord God of Israel,*
for he has visited and redeemed his people
⁶⁹ *and has raised up a horn of salvation for us*
in the house of his servant David,
⁷⁰ *as he spoke by the mouth of his holy prophets from of old,*
⁷¹ *that we should be saved from our enemies*
and from the hand of all who hate us;
⁷² *to show the mercy promised to our fathers*
and to remember his holy covenant,
⁷³ *the oath that he swore to our father Abraham, to grant us*
⁷⁴ *that we, being delivered from the hand of our enemies,*
might serve him without fear,
⁷⁵ *in holiness and righteousness before him all our days.*
⁷⁶ *And you, child, will be called the prophet of the Most High;*
for you will go before the Lord to prepare his ways,
⁷⁷ *to give knowledge of salvation to his people*

in the forgiveness of their sins,
78 because of the tender mercy of our God,
whereby the sunrise shall visit us from on high
79 to give light to those who sit in darkness and in the shadow of
death, to guide our feet into the way of peace."

80 And the child grew and became strong in spirit, and he was in
the wilderness until the day of his public appearance to Israel.
(ESV)

In Zechariah's prophecy, he recalls and claims the promises of God passed through the generations from *"holy prophets of old."* With the impending birth of the Messiah, Israel will be saved from their enemies, receive the Lord's mercy, and be able to serve the Lord without fear.

However, the real wonder of this prophecy exists in the latter half, as Zechariah speaks to his newborn son, and it is worth repeating.

"And you, child, will be called the prophet of the Most High; for you will go before the Lord to prepare the way for Him, to give his people the knowledge of salvation through the forgiveness of their sins, because of the tender mercy of our God, by which the rising sun will come to us from heaven to shine on those living in the darkness and in the shadow of death, to guide our feet into the path of peace."

Zechariah spoke these words when John was eight days old. Nearly 30 years later, God would fulfill them in this child, who *"grew and became strong in spirit"* and lived *"in the wilderness until the day of his public appearance to Israel."*

A Prayer for Today

~

Lord God, every word You have spoken has or will come to pass, even as it did with Zechariah's prophecy about the coming Messiah and John's role in preparing the way for Him. Your mercy and deliverance are still available today for those who do not know you. May I be a "voice in the wilderness" like John, proclaiming the salvation of the Lord.

LUKE 2:1-7

THE WONDER OF THE IMPOSSIBLE

¹ In those days Caesar Augustus issued a decree that a census should be taken of the entire Roman world. ² (This was the first census that took place while Quirinius was governor of Syria.) ³ And everyone went to their own town to register.

⁴ So Joseph also went up from the town of Nazareth in Galilee to Judea, to Bethlehem the town of David, because he belonged to the house and line of David. ⁵ He went there to register with Mary, who was pledged to be married to him and was expecting a child. ⁶ While they were there, the time came for the baby to be born, ⁷ and she gave birth to her firstborn, a son. She wrapped him in cloths and placed him in a manger, because there was no guest room available for them.

If Caesar Augustus had not issued the decree for a census at that exact time in history, Joseph would never have taken Mary to Bethlehem when she was nine months pregnant. Jesus would have been born in Nazareth, and his birthplace alone (which he had no control over) would have discredited his claim to be the Christ. In Micah 5:2, it states that the Messiah will come from Bethlehem: *"But you, Bethlehem Ephrathah, though you are small among the clans of Judah, out of you will come for me one who will be ruler over Israel, whose origins are from of old, from ancient times."*

This is just the first of several prophecies fulfilled through no deliberate action by Jesus. If Joseph had rejected Mary, as was well within his right to do, the line of David leading to the Messiah would not have been established. There are a multitude of "what if's" that could have thwarted God's plan. As we have seen time and again, though, there is nothing that can stop the plans or promises of God.

The very idea of Mary, nine months pregnant, trekking the 100-mile journey from Nazareth to Bethlehem on a donkey is nearly unfathomable. Exhausted, they finally arrive, only to find there is no place for them to stay, and Mary is beginning to experience birth pangs. I can't help but wonder if there was no room for them not only because of the crowding from the census but also because of the ignominy of Mary's condition (despite the fact that she and Joseph were married). Whether out of mercy or judgment, the only place offered to Mary and Joseph was a dirty, unsanitary, animal-filled stable.

Young Mary, experiencing childbirth for the first time with only Joseph the carpenter and some common barn animals at her side, delivered her firstborn Son, the Savior of the world. How simply the act is described. *"She wrapped him in cloths"*—like all mothers do—and *"laid him in a manger"*—like no mothers do—*"for there was no guest room available for them."* Women today have either the luxury of sterilized, hotel-like hospital rooms or the comforts of home—both with qualified professionals on hand—in which to bring our children into the world. Mary had a bed of coarse straw, the company of a clueless man, and a barn full of animals among which to deliver her son. She probably felt much like an animal herself while in the primal rites of birth.

Did the Lord lessen her pain, shorten her labor, prevent her from tearing (who would sew her up)? How did they cut the umbilical cord? Where did they get the cloths and water needed to clean up after the birth? How did they keep the delivery of Jesus free from contact with the dirty straw and animal germs?

Such an un-royal birth. Such a brave young woman and steadfast man. Such a relief that all went smoothly and without incident. What a strange and miraculous moment within the confines of a common stable to be the first ones to behold the Son of God.

A Prayer for Today

~

"O Sovereign LORD! You made the heavens and earth by your strong hand and powerful arm. Nothing is too hard for you!" (Jer. 32:17, NLT) Like Jeremiah, I cannot help but see Your divine providence as I read this account. How can I help but put my trust in the One who makes all things come to pass according to His Word and promise? As Jesus states later in Luke, "What is impossible with man is possible with God." I want to live in the realm of the impossible, by faith, where I can see You more clearly. Thank You for being greater than my circumstances, for making a way where there seems to be no way.

LUKE 2:8-15

THE WONDER OF GOD'S GLORY

8 And there were shepherds living out in the fields nearby, keeping watch over their flocks at night. 9 An angel of the Lord appeared to them, and the glory of the Lord shone around them, and they were terrified. 10 But the angel said to them, "Do not be afraid. I bring you good news that will cause great joy for all the people. 11 Today in the town of David a Savior has been born to you; he is the Messiah, the Lord. 12 This will be a sign to you: You will find a baby wrapped in cloths and lying in a manger."

13 Suddenly a great company of the heavenly host appeared with the angel, praising God and saying,

14 "Glory to God in the highest heaven,
and on earth peace to those on whom his favor rests."

15 When the angels had left them and gone into heaven, the shepherds said to one another, "Let's go to Bethlehem and see this thing that has happened, which the Lord has told us about."

Much like Zechariah and Mary, the shepherds were simply going about their daily business. Suddenly, an angel appeared to them in the darkness, *and* the glory of the Lord shone around them! Like Zechariah and Mary, they too were afraid —terrified!—and the angel also encouraged them not to fear. *"I bring you good news that will cause great joy for all the people."* These common shepherds were the first outsiders to hear of the Savior's birth. God continues to choose the lowly and the humble to accomplish His purposes today.

If seeing one angel is terrifying, what would it be like to see a *"great company of the heavenly host"?* Better than any fireworks display, laser show, or modern-day special effects, I'll bet. They materialize out of nowhere, for the express purpose of proclaiming praise to God. Then, just as quickly as they appeared, they vanish from sight.

The sky darkens once more, and the shepherds look at each other and say, "Let's go to Bethlehem!"

A Prayer for Today

~

Lord, I cannot begin to wrap my head around this incredible moment. To see Your heavenly host of angels appear in the sky, to have the glory of the Lord shine around me is simply unfathomable! What these shepherds saw that night changed their lives forever. Encountering the glory of God was not just for them, though. I can experience Your glory, too, through the gift of salvation and a life lived in accordance with your Word and the Holy Spirit. Show me Your glory, Lord.

LUKE 2:16-20

THE WONDER OF THE GOOD NEWS

16 So they hurried off and found Mary and Joseph, and the baby, who was lying in the manger. 17 When they had seen him, they spread the word concerning what had been told them about this child, 18 and all who heard it were amazed at what the shepherds said to them. 19 But Mary treasured up all these things and pondered them in her heart. 20 The shepherds returned, glorifying and praising God for all the things they had heard and seen, which were just as they had been told.

I love the pure faith of these shepherds which propels them to hurry into town, leaving their sheep behind. There is no wonder like the glory of God breaking into our world. What a surprise it must have been when these unkempt, dirty shepherds suddenly showed up at the stable. Their faces aglow with anticipation, they approach the manger and stare in awe at the face of their Savior.

An angelic visitation and the sight of the baby was all it took to transform these shepherds into evangelists that night. They became the first disciples, leaving everything to find the Savior and tell others about Him.

As for Mary, *"she treasured up all these things and pondered them in*

47

her heart." For those of us who are mothers, think back to those first, treasured moments with your own newborn. Every feature, every movement, every sound is beautiful, miraculous, and perfect. Mary has just given birth, through divine conception, to the Savior of the world. As she watches him resting peacefully in the manger—her pain forgotten in the glory of new life—news of His arrival begins to trickle in from the outside. Bedraggled shepherds are the first to come and worship and then go out to spread the word, "The Messiah has been born!" So much to take in for a young girl, so much in store for this tiny baby, her son and Savior.

A Prayer for Today

Lord Jesus, I want my life to be forever changed by the Good News the shepherds proclaimed that night. I have a Savior, and He is the Christ! I want my lips to be overflowing with Your praise such that I cannot help but share the hope I have within me. You are too wonderful to keep to myself, Jesus!

LUKE 2:21-35

THE WONDER OF PROMISES FULFILLED

21 On the eighth day, when it was time to circumcise the child, he was named Jesus, the name the angel had given him before he was conceived.

22 When the time came for the purification rites required by the Law of Moses, Joseph and Mary took him to Jerusalem to present him to the Lord 23 (as it is written in the Law of the Lord, "Every firstborn male is to be consecrated to the Lord"), 24 and to offer a sacrifice in keeping with what is said in the Law of the Lord: "a pair of doves or two young pigeons."

25 Now there was a man in Jerusalem called Simeon, who was righteous and devout. He was waiting for the consolation of Israel, and the Holy Spirit was on him. 26 It had been revealed to him by the Holy Spirit that he would not die before he had seen the Lord's Messiah. 27 Moved by the Spirit, he went into the temple courts. When the parents brought in the child Jesus to do for him what the custom of the Law required, 28 Simeon took him in his arms and praised God, saying:

29 "Sovereign Lord, as you have promised,

you may now dismiss your servant in peace.
30 For my eyes have seen your salvation,
31 which you have prepared in the sight of all nations:
32 a light for revelation to the Gentiles,
and the glory of your people Israel."

33 The child's father and mother marveled at what was said about him. 34 Then Simeon blessed them and said to Mary, his mother: "This child is destined to cause the falling and rising of many in Israel, and to be a sign that will be spoken against, 35 so that the thoughts of many hearts will be revealed. And a sword will pierce your own soul too."

Joseph and Mary obeyed the law of the Lord, bringing their baby for the purification rites, which included circumcision and naming him Jesus, as Gabriel had instructed them to do.

Imagine going to consecrate your first child to the Lord. Already, Joseph and Mary have experienced so much: encounters with the angel, Elizabeth, Jesus, and the shepherds. Now, as they enter the temple, a wizened old man approaches them. He takes Jesus in his feeble arms and proclaims praise to God. He prophesies that this baby is salvation—*"a light for revelation to the Gentiles, and the glory of your people Israel."* Jesus has come for all, not just for one people group.

What is remarkable about this old man named Simeon is that he, too, had received a promise from God: he would get to see the Messiah before he died. The Holy Spirit led him into the temple that day, in time to see Jesus, his Messiah. That is all Simeon had been living for in his advanced age, and oh, the joy he must have felt upon holding that baby in his arms and looking into his wonderful face! *"You may now dismiss your servant in peace,"* he says. His life was made complete that day. The Lord rewarded him for his faithfulness in the most magnificent way.

Does it surprise you that Joseph and Mary marveled at

Simeon's words? Despite all the evidence pointing to the fact that their baby was indeed the Messiah, it must have still seemed surreal to have people keep entering their lives and confirming its truth.

Simeon blesses Joseph and Mary. Then he leans in and, as he places the baby in Mary's arms, he prophesies the darker half of Jesus' mission on this earth: the revealing of sinful hearts, the trouble for Israel, the division his name will cause. He ends with, *"And a sword will pierce your own soul, too."*

Mary was a thoughtful young woman. I don't think she was prone to superstition or frivolity. I'll bet she kept this little nugget of truth tucked away in her heart, pondering what it would mean for her throughout Jesus' life. She later experienced the fullness of it when the sword pierced Jesus' side as He hung on the cross, and she watched his blood and water flow out.

Perhaps these words were spoken to make it clear to Mary (and those who would come after her) that she, too, was a sinner. The truth of who Jesus was and His teachings would pierce her heart with the awareness of her sin and need for a Savior. Before she had time to discern the meaning behind Simeon's words, though, another person approached her and Joseph.

A Prayer for Today

∾

Lord God, Your Word says that *"all have sinned and fallen short of the glory of God."* (Rom 3:23) Thank you for providing Jesus, Savior of both the Jews and the Gentiles. Thank You for fulfilling Your promises, from Adam all the way to Simeon (and beyond). Your Word is trustworthy and true.

LUKE 2:36-40

THE WONDER OF A WOMAN OF GOD

³⁶ There was also a prophet, Anna, the daughter of Penuel, of the tribe of Asher. She was very old; she had lived with her husband seven years after her marriage, ³⁷ and then was a widow until she was eighty-four. She never left the temple but worshiped night and day, fasting and praying. ³⁸ Coming up to them at that very moment, she gave thanks to God and spoke about the child to all who were looking forward to the redemption of Jerusalem.

³⁹ When Joseph and Mary had done everything required by the Law of the Lord, they returned to Galilee to their own town of Nazareth. ⁴⁰ And the child grew and became strong; he was filled with wisdom, and the grace of God was on him.

Just as Simeon finishes prophesying, Anna approaches Joseph and Mary. Anna is a rare character in the bible, a female prophet. After seven years of marriage, she became a widow, and has spent the rest of her life worshipping, fasting, and praying in the temple, where she lived, waiting for this one divine moment when she would fulfill her calling as a prophet.

Standing before Joseph and Mary, she gives thanks to God for their baby. She later shares the news of Jesus with all *"who were looking forward to the redemption of Jerusalem."* I love how God singled out this older woman, giving her a name and place in history. She must have been a remarkable woman of God.

A Prayer for Today

~

Lord Jesus, the life of Anna inspires me to be more committed in my own relationship with You. She lived most of her life in dedicated worship and prayer. I know that I have daily responsibilities to perform and so many distractions, but help me to remember that I can continually pray and worship throughout the day. Let my prayers be like the breaths I take: spontaneous, instinctive, and natural. I want to be in constant communion with You. I want to be a wonder-ful woman (or man) of God.

CONCLUSION

What a whirlwind journey this was for Joseph and Mary! They traveled to Bethlehem, gave birth to Jesus in a dirty stable, were approached by poor, unkempt shepherds, and then approached by a wizened old man and prophetess. Each strange encounter further solidified their faith in the promise God had made: their son was indeed the Savior of the world.

There are so many unanswered questions, though, about this incredible week they experienced. Did they live in the stable those first eight days? Did a midwife or local woman come to help Mary care for Jesus—to show her how to nurse him, swaddle him, change him? Did they receive blankets or clean cloths to wrap him in? There is no talk of that first week: the sleeplessness, the uncertainty, the joy.

Perhaps God did for Mary and Joseph as He recently did for friends of mine. They were forced to leave their home and had nowhere to stay (with six children!). God provided them with a temporary home (in Hawaii, no less!), and protected them on their adventure from Wisconsin to Washington. He made a way where there seemed to be no way, going above and beyond for them, and all because they choose to live with open hands and faithful hearts to Him.

I like to think that God showered Mary and Joseph and Jesus with all their needs and added blessings besides. This way, when they took Jesus to be consecrated to the Lord (faithfully following the Law of the Lord), they too came with open hearts, clean bodies, and peaceful minds that were ready to hear the good news proclaimed by both Simeon and Anna.

For the next 12 years, we can only guess at Jesus' boyhood. Was he a quiet, studious boy, his head always bent over a scroll? Or, was he active and boisterous, always running out to play with his neighborhood buddies? Did he love to stand beside Joseph and hand him his tools until he was old enough to join in the work, or was he a bit bungling and awkward? We don't know the details, but we are given a brief character sketch of this growing boy at the end of Luke chapter two: *"He grew and became strong; he was filled with wisdom and the grace of God was upon him."* Through the love of his family and the divine purpose of his heavenly Father, Jesus grew into a physically, mentally, and spiritually well-rounded young man.

How can we live like the characters in Christ's birth story, with simple faith and obedience to God's will? At so many points along the way, God's name could have been discredited by the choices of the people He invited to be part of His plan. However, as we have seen throughout these two chapters alone, God holds all things in His hands, and His purposes and promises will always prevail. As it says in Proverbs 19:21, *"Many are the plans in a person's heart, but it is the Lord's purpose that prevails."*

Oswald Chambers explains it further: "The circumstances of a man's life are ordained by God. In the life of a saint there is no chance. God by His providence brings you into circumstances that you cannot understand at all, but the Spirit of God understands. God brings you to places, among people, and into certain conditions to accomplish a definite purpose through the intercession of the Spirit in you."‡

What purpose has God ordained for you?

My hope is that you will seek it out in His Word, through prayer, and by obedience to the Holy Spirit. I pray that your life will be filled with the wonder of the One who came to this earth to—as my pastor often says—"live the perfect life you could never live and die the death you would never want to die," in order to give you eternal life, a glorious hope, and a rich, personal relationship with God.

Thank you, Jesus!

RESOURCES

• All verses taken from the New International Version except as indicated within the text
• † Bryant, Evans. "Who Is Theophilus?"
http://preachersstudyblog.com.
Last modified October 11, 2011.
http://preachersstudyblog.com/2011/10/who-is-theophilus/.
• ‡ Chambers, Oswald *My Utmost for His Highest*.
Barbour Publishing, Inc., 1935; 1963.
• § https://biblehub.com/commentaries/luke/1-9.htm

All images courtesy of Unsplash.com:
Snowflake cover image by Aaron Burden
Middle East image by Sergey Pesterev
Incense image by Ramakrishnan Nataraj
Angel image by Kasper Rasmussen
Pregnancy image by Arteida MjESHTRI
Manger image by Greyson Joralemon
Sheep image by Jaka Skerlep
Bible image by Aaron Burden

ABOUT THE AUTHOR

Aimee Mae Wiley is a freelance writer and editor whose work can be found in the Chicken Soup for the Soul series, among other publications. She blogs at Whispers of Worth about her passion for simplicity and surrender.

She and her husband reside in Cedarburg, Wisconsin with their five children.

Connect with Aimee online at
www.whispersofworth.com

Made in the USA
Columbia, SC
17 November 2019